How We Survived A Pandemic As Entrepreneurs

Follow Our Leads

Book 4

By James Lott, Jr And Cesar R Espino

Also by James Lott Jr and Cesar R Espino:

Follow Our Leads Book 1: How We Became Entrepreneurs

Follow Our Leads Book 2: What It's Like Being Entrepreneurs

Follow Our Leads Book 3: How We Stay Entrepreneurs

And from Cesar R Espino (featuring James Lott Jr)

You Can Overcome Anything Volume 1:Despite The Barriers In Life

You Can Overcome Anything Volume 10: With Awareness

James Lott Jr

Unexpected Times

"Will you make me throw everything away" is the first question many prospective clients ask me during our first consultation. OF course the answer is NO. It would be like going to the Dentist and asking him to extract all your teeth so you won't get cavities anymore. Absurd, right. Being A Certified Professional Organizer AND Certified Life Coach with Specialties in Organization, I start with the mind and the heart. Those two are VERY important to getting organized and STAYING that way.

The mind and the heart fuel the various reasons people become cluttered and have a hard time letting go of items. In my 14 years of practice, I've noticed that the root cause is almost always an event that affects a person traumatically. Some example's from clients, "my mother died when I was 16 and she loved turtles." Cut to present day and the client is 40 and has bought so many items with turtles on them you can't see the living room floor or couches. "My father lost his job when I was 9 and we were super poor after that."

4

Now the client is 60 and has so many paper plates and plastic utensils to fill 2 rooms. Some will call it "collecting". Others will say, you can't see it, it's all put away." But if you open a drawer or closet, it would resemble a cartoon of everything falling out. Before you can start, you have to identify where the issue started.

As the Super Organizer, My motto is "Small Steps Leads To Large Rewards." What that means for me is essentially every step is a step. To walk forward, you have to move your legs but does it matter how big the step is….no…as long as you keep stepping, you will move forward. Organizing a cluttered room is similar to organizing a cluttered mind. At first the clutter is too large to comprehend and attack, so the best thing is to start small, handle the small areas first.

First you have to admit that there is an issue and without blame, guilt or shame, acknowledge its presence and vow to change it. Next you come up with a plan to start. I will use the cluttered room as the focus. As you try to walk into the room, the door nearly opens all the way, so you start there. You say, "I will just work on clearing the stuff behind the door." You look and its 3 or 4 large items that clearly don't belong there that are preventing the door from opening completely.

YOU pull those things out. 2 of them are broken and old, so you throw those out.

The third thing is something you've been meaning to give to your niece. SO you put that in your car to give to your niece when you see her this Sunday at the family dinner. Then you vacuum behind there and you're done!
The door opens fully and you LITERALLY opened the door to a new lease on life!

In 2019, I was busy with Organizing clients and life coaching clients. I had a partnership with Michaels (yes THAT Michaels) where I taught classes using their organization products. I was teaching classes on my own too. I was doing media at AfterbuzzTV!

Then 2020 came…

When I look back, one of the main things I got out of that time for me and many others is:

It was a reset button on my business.

The COVID-19 pandemic, which swept across the globe starting in 2020, had a profound impact on societies, economies, and businesses.

While the pandemic presented immense challenges and disruptions, it also served as a reset button for many entrepreneurs. Forced to adapt to new circumstances, entrepreneurs found themselves reinventing their businesses, discovering innovative solutions, and seizing new opportunities.

In this book, we explore how the COVID-19 pandemic became a catalyst for change, prompting myself (and Cesar) to reset their strategies, reevaluate their goals, and embrace transformative growth.

1. Necessity Breeds Innovation:
During the pandemic, entrepreneurs faced unprecedented challenges as traditional business models were upended by lockdowns, supply chain disruptions, and changing consumer behaviors. Many businesses were on the verge of collapse, prompting entrepreneurs to think creatively and adapt swiftly to survive.

This necessity led to a wave of innovation, with entrepreneurs developing new products, services, and business models to meet the changing needs of customers. Startups emerged in various sectors, including healthcare technology, remote work solutions, e-commerce, and contactless delivery services. The pandemic compelled entrepreneurs to explore uncharted territories and reimagine their businesses from the ground up.

2. Embracing Digital Transformation:
The pandemic accelerated the digital transformation of businesses across industries. Entrepreneurs who had previously been hesitant or slow to embrace technology suddenly found themselves with no choice but to pivot towards digital solutions. This shift led to the rise of online platforms, remote work tools, virtual events, and e-commerce initiatives.

Entrepreneurs quickly adapted their operations to leverage technology, streamline processes, and improve efficiency. As a result, many businesses discovered the advantages of remote work, online sales channels, and data-driven decision-making. The pandemic acted as a catalyst, propelling entrepreneurs into the digital age and opening up new avenues for growth.

3. Focus on Social Impact:
The pandemic highlighted the importance of social responsibility and community support. Entrepreneurs recognized the need to contribute to the well-being of society and stepped up to address critical issues arising from the crisis. Many businesses shifted their production lines to manufacture essential medical supplies, donated resources to healthcare institutions, or provided free services to those in need.

The pandemic served as a reminder that entrepreneurs have a role beyond profit-making and that businesses can be powerful forces for positive change. Entrepreneurs who reset their mindset to prioritize social impact found new purpose and strengthened their relationships with customers and communities.

4. Reevaluating Business Models and Priorities:
The pandemic compelled entrepreneurs to take a hard look at their business models, strategies, and long-term goals. Many realized that their previous assumptions and plans were no longer viable in the new normal. As a result, entrepreneurs embarked on a process of reevaluation, analyzing market trends, consumer behaviors, and emerging opportunities.

Some chose to pivot their business entirely, entering new industries or niches that were thriving amidst the pandemic. Others focused on diversifying their revenue streams or exploring strategic partnerships to navigate uncertainty. The pandemic became a turning point, prompting entrepreneurs to reassess their priorities and reshape their businesses accordingly.

The COVID-19 pandemic was a disruptive force that upended economies and societies worldwide. However, amidst the challenges, it also served as a reset button for many entrepreneurs. The need to adapt, innovate, and address emerging needs forced entrepreneurs to redefine their businesses, embrace digital transformation, and prioritize social impact.

The pandemic compelled entrepreneurs to reassess their strategies, reimagine their goals, and find opportunities within the chaos. As a result, we have witnessed a surge of entrepreneurial resilience, creativity, and adaptability that will shape the business landscape for years to come.

And all of that is and was true for me!

I embarked on a journey to build my media empire amidst the chaos and uncertainty of the pandemic. As an entrepreneur and media personality, I was determined to turn adversity into opportunity and make a lasting impact in the industry.

Even before the pandemic hit, I had already established myself as a respected figure in the media world.

With years of experience in radio, television, and podcasting, I had a solid foundation to build upon. But when the world came to a standstill, I knew I had to adapt and find new ways to connect with my audience.

Recognizing the immense potential of the digital landscape, I quickly shifted my focus to online platforms. Social media, streaming services, and virtual communication became my primary tools for expanding my reach and engaging with my fans. It was a bold move, but I knew it was the right direction to take.

One of my first ventures during the pandemic was the creation of the JLJ Media NETWORK , a podcast network that aimed to entertain and enlighten. Leveraging my industry connections and expertise, I brought together a talented team of hosts and launched a diverse range of shows covering everything from entertainment to self-help.

The response was overwhelming!

Our audience grew rapidly, and we gained attention from industry insiders who recognized the innovative approach we were taking.
But I didn't stop there. I saw the increasing demand for virtual events and online conferences, and I seized the opportunity. I organized and hosted numerous digital summits and panels, bringing together experts, influencers, and celebrities from various fields. These events not only provided valuable insights but also fostered meaningful connections within the industry.

Which continues to come in handy today!

Expanding my media empire, I ventured into producing and directing original content. Streaming platforms became my canvas, and I created a web series that showcased emerging talent and shed light on important social issues. Through this platform, I aimed to amplify underrepresented voices and promote inclusivity and diversity in the media landscape.

I went on to use both sides of my brain and created and written audio dramas, music, video series and more. Utilized the talent on my network and showcased their shows and ideas too.

No one is an island!

Throughout this journey, my dedication to my craft and my unwavering work ethic remained constant. I embraced new technologies and platforms, staying true to my authentic voice and vision. Connecting with my audience on a personal level and sharing compelling stories became the cornerstone of my success.

I also increased my revenue and my streams of income. In some cases one project would pay me in 2 or 3 different ways!

The achievements I made during the pandemic serve as a testament to the resilience and creativity that individuals possess in the face of adversity. I am proud to have built a media empire that resonates with audiences worldwide, even during the most challenging times. As the media landscape continues to evolve, I hope my story inspires aspiring media entrepreneurs to follow their passions and leave their mark in the digital era.

Building my media empire during the pandemic was a transformative experience. It taught me the importance of adaptability, innovation, and staying true to my vision. I am excited to continue this journey, connecting with audiences and making a positive impact in the media industry for years to come.

linkedin.com/jameslottjr

alottofhelp.com

Cesar R Espino

Thriving on Challenging Times

Oh boy! it is the end of 2019, and I am excited and at the same time not knowing what to expect. That is exactly what I was thinking as 2020 was fast approaching, and that is because it was a milestone with a "Zero" at the end of the year in my life. No, I do not say it because the year was going to be 202**0**, I say it because that is the year, I was turning 4**0**.

I remember telling every one of my friends, those who were entrepreneurs and those who had their 9-5 JOB that I had known for a while that we should all come together and do a destination trip to celebrate my birthday. The funny thing is that I had so many friends that said they would for sure do something and join the fun and that got me so happy. As we entered the new year, I was super excited for the new level I was entering, and to be exact my birthday is January 27th, and I had decided I wanted to celebrate my birthday in Los Cabos San Lucas with all my friends.

By this year I was going on two years (actually one year and a half) of being a full-time entrepreneur, and talk about taking a leap of faith, that was scary. Yet I was making and that was due to having a target plan, a vision, and a desire to become greater than who I was.

As we got closer to my birthday I reached out to everyone who said will join me in Cabos San Lucas for my birthday, and well you remember how I said it was funny I had a great response, well in the contrary no one responded and I had already book my trip and I was not expecting anyone to show up and it will be just me. Yet I was determined that I was going to take this trip with out without anyone and enjoy my time. This by itself is a lesson because often time as entrepreneurs and or more importantly as people we tend to walk on a lonely path, and to reach greatness we must walk alone for a while. On top of that we only live once and we have to make the best out of it with or without people and cannot wait for other approval or for others to brings us joy. And with that I've decided I will do this for me and enjoy my birthday.

To my surprise some friends (a couple and their son) who I've met at a self-development event and who live in Norther California (I live in Southern California) actually showed up and their layover was at LAX (Los Angeles International Airport) and our flight to Los Cabos San Lucas was the same flight out of LAX to Mexico. This brought me so much joy because they joined me in my birthday celebration and they actually showed up for me. I must tell you this is a moment in life I will never forget, and I am beyond grateful for them and to this date, they are still really great friends. As a matter of fact in 2022 they got legally married in Florence Italy and I made a point to be there fore them, besides the fact that I was part of the groomsmen party.

By this time we were having such a great time celebrating my birthday in Mexico (Los Cabos San Lucas) without even realizing that the world was going through some transformation. You see, as an entrepreneur and when I've decided to embark on this journey, if you have read one of the previous books of this series, and if not you should, I really do not watch news, because news are not good in my eyes they are just bad news and bad programming (not something you need in your life, let alone let others program you and dictate what to do and or bring fear to you) and the react. I had decided to give up news or watch them, I figure if there is something so important and or critical I will hear that from close friends who are at the same level as I am, that level of growth, self-development, discipline, and who want more out of life.

Having that said, I was enjoying my time, my 40th birthday not knowing what was really going on with the world or what was to come. Soon my 7-day vacation and the joy of spending time with my friends was coming to an end, by this time there were still no real signs of restrictions imposed by our "so call government", and we all were preparing to go back to our homes.

Well, to a certain extent I wish that was not the case because as soon as I got back to Los Angeles, I remember getting this news that the country was going through some shutdowns, and the world was going into panic.

I never saw this happen and as an entrepreneur three of my businesses got affected, and by the way I believe that you need to have multiple streams of income as an entrepreneur.

Besides my businesses getting affected (real estate investing, business consulting, event coaching and back of the room sales), Los Angeles, like many other areas of the United States like the entire world was going through its own challenges. Challenges like shortage of supplies, toilet paper, water, food, and other stuff, like riots, break ins, and people going insane. All these things were chaotic, and honestly the world was not ready for this type of change.

Many businesses were forced to close down, some were forced to keep their employees at a distance and away from the work place and secluded and contained in their houses. In my opinion this was just another form of programming for the government or those who had the buying power to control humankind, that in itself is another book, and while I do not expect for you to believe in my points of views I cannot stay away from facts and reality.

Nevertheless, we were all secluded from even going to gather at church, or celebrate a family birthday or special occasion, and or even go out in public and enjoy an nice meal. For God's sake it was the beginning of drive through celebration for graduation and or birthday celebration, how crazy is that?

Regardless of that negative programming and madness, many people were force out of a job and unemployment was on their high from many years, and specially people like me, entrepreneurs who did not pivot, did not react, and or were just starting had no other choice, and leave that dream and go many steps backs.

Yet I knew that could not be me, I will not put myself in that category, I had come so far and gone through so much to just give up, so I pivot. My real estate investing business slowed down, because people were so afraid of all the things they heard on the news and were not selling. My live events that I will coach and do back of the room sales were being cancelled because we were forced to not have gatherings, and my business consulting business also hurt as the employer had to have their employees work from home, and due to the fear COVID imposed they did not want to see me frequently and our zoom or virtual meetings were limited. I have to tell you I've lost a lot, and being a full-time entrepreneur going into 2020 just under two years was not promising and fear, discomfort, the unknown was creeping in.

Instead of giving up I had to think, I had to look at other possible strategies, and I had to pivot. As one of my mentors said, "deal with what emerges", and so I did. At the beginning of 2020 I begun a new hobby, which with the pandemic turned into a quick strategy, and that is the birth of my Podcast Show, called You Can Overcome Anything! Podcast Show!

On February 2020 and with much free time I decided to start a podcast that will bring people together from all walks of life to inspire, empower, and motivate. And so I embarked on this new hobby and mission. My objective was to bring people all over the world and allow others to learn and listen and get connected with the different stories so they can learn, pivot, and act, especially during the pandemic.

While this began as a hobby, I found myself learning and taking in so much information that will also allow me to reflect, act, and do.

And several things that were needed during the pandemic was to reflect, act and do, and while many of us fun ourselves with plenty of our time, one thing I've learned is that those that prevail did not just got busy with useless things, or allowed time to pass them by, yet they utilized the extra time to crate something new. One of the things I've talked about in my early on podcast was that for one to flourish, and growth, needed to utilized the time they had on their hands to grow and evolved. Even to this date, anyone looking to get to that next level has to look deep down and see how they best utilized their time. At the end we will have the same amount of time, no matter if you are a billionaire or just making it, we all have the same amount of time. The difference is what we do with our time. It reminds me of what Les Brown said "if you do what it is easy your life will be easy, and if you do what is hard your life will be easy. When you think of this, it is easy to not do anything and look at a Netflix show, or it is easy to eat that pizza, or it is easy to cheap on your husband or wife, yet at the end your life is for sure to be hard.

How is that, well not having the means, being overweight and having health complications, going through a difficult breakup relationship and worse hurting another person. Now if you do what is hard, such as working on a business idea, turning off the tv, working out, making the best of your relationship even when you feel there is no hope. What do you get, you get to be on the other side of that tunnel with a great business idea, financial freedom or better than where you are today. Having a fit body, yet more importantly being sick free, and having a loving, passionate relationship, or even way better a relationship with oneself.

As part of my entrepreneurial journey and even going through the pandemic I focus a lot on reading and listening to other successful and motivational people, and if you are going through some challenges now, you must do this, believe me this will help you and give you the strength and ideas to keep moving forward, and as I said help you get 1% better then who you were yesterday. So another speaker I listened to a lot is Jim Rohn, and one thing that resonated with me that he said is "that for things to change, you have to change".

No matter what was going on in politics, the world, your community or any external part, for things to change you have to change from the inside out. This was critical during the pandemic, because I had all the answers, and those that survive had to get created and discovered something new and different that perhaps they did not think they had. Often times we discover some talents when we are being faced with some difficulty.

2020, when I believe this whole pandemic started was pivotal moment for me, as not only did I began something new, I had to look deep down on my businesses and had to look at how I can pivot, how can I bring more value, and how can I strategies to make sure I continue to grow vs fall back down. The key here was asking "how" and not "why" this is happening to me. From this another great idea grew and in quarter 3 of 2020 I came up with a new concept that I knew I can capitalize on, help many people all over the world, and help others get their voice heard.

I was already many episodes on my podcast show, doing about three new episodes per week, as I had many people wanting to get interview and because of the demand, I was interviewing people and their interview was not airing until 3 months later from their interview. With my podcast show came the idea of creating another form of communication also bringing people from all walks of life, sharing, inspiring, motivating, and empowering many through very specific topics.

So, I embarked in creating and giving the ability for many people to become published author through a collaboration book project, called You Can Overcome Anything. My very first volume I had a total of 16 people join, to include my very own daughter. Not only did this create an opportunity for people to share a story and have the entire world hear that story, it also gave faith and hope to those who were reading the book. During the pandemic people needed hope and were seeking external advice to help them keep moving forward. On top of that it created a new business idea for me to not only help me get more eyes on me, get more publicity, a new income stream, and best of all guidance in my own life, as I too learn from each and everyone's story.

This first volume of You Can Overcome Anything was a success, and being able to think outside the box during a pandemic was by far a complete success. The lesson here is that no matter what you are facing, or what is going around your surroundings, you need to put some time aside, concentrate, ask, and be willing to received as many ideas as possible and while you may not have all the answers, begin at once with what you have, the worse that could happen is it did not work, yet the best thing that could happen is that it was a total success. And while we always have to see how we can get better, you must review, rehearse, and revise everything you do. And as such I have done that with both my podcast and my book series.

Take for instance from my podcast I have gain clients for some of my other businesses I have, and I have also gain business partners that will invest with me on real estate. While on the other hand with the book series, I have grown that to now going on Vol. 11, with over 90 people from all over the world, from Canada, USA, Mexico, Australia, and most recently from Nigeria that have become Amazon bestseller in multiple categories.

This has become a business in its own helping people fulfill their dream of becoming a published author and at the same time helping others. And now this has also become a new business idea in the middle of 2022 with now helping people write their own book, becoming a bestseller and giving them that creditability they are looking for to continue to grow their name and brand.

Whether you want to level up during a pandemic, a financial crises, a political year, or whatever else life throws at you, you need to first have the desire to not give up, second you need to relax, think, and ask what else can you do that will make a difference in someone's life, and above all belief in you, believe that you can make a difference, and you can do it. And as an African proverb says, "If there is no enemy within, the enemy outside can do us no harm". Never forget that you can, you will, and you must.

www.CesarRespino.com

www.linktree.com/espinoc

From James Lott Jr & Cesar R Espino:

Thank you for your support by picking up this book and any of the others in this series. We believe in YOU. We are sharing our experiences in a realistic way and hopefully you are able to gain insight for YOU.

This isn't one way or path.

Mail- James Lott Jr

JLJ Media

8939 S Sepulveda Suite 110

#339

Los Angeles CA 90045

@2024 JLJ Media

www.ingramcontent.com/pod-product-compliance
Lightning Source LLC
Chambersburg PA
CBHW082242220526
45479CB00005B/1315